Bumblebees

by Sara van Dyck

Lerner Publications Company • Minneapolis

The author is most grateful to all those who contributed to this book. Special thanks go to Stephen Buchmann, Ph.D., Associate Professor of Entomology, the University of Arizona, and founder of the Bee Works in Tucson, Arizona, who inspired the book and shared his extensive knowledge of native bees; and Brent Karner, coordinator of the Insect Zoo of the Natural History Museum of Los Angeles County, who generously gave his time to help with research and writing.

Photographs are reproduced with the permission of: © Steve Kaufman/CORBIS, cover; © Dwight R. Kuhn, pp. 4, 6, 8, 9, 10, 11, 13, 14, 15, 16, 17, 18, 20, 21, 23, 24, 25, 26, 27, 28, 29, 30, 31, 32, 33, 34, 35, 36, 37, 38, 39, 43; © Treat Davidson; Frank Lane Picture Agency/CORBIS, p. 7; © Gray Hardel/CORBIS, p. 12; PhotoDisc Royalty Free by Getty Images, pp. 19, 40; Hubert Stadler/CORBIS, p. 22; © Steve Terrill/CORBIS, p. 41; © Paul A. Souders/ CORBIS, p. 42; © Ken Wilson; Papilio/CORBIS, pp. 46–47.

Lerner Publications Company
A division of Lerner Publishing Group
241 First Avenue North
Minneapolis, MN 55401 U.S.A.

Website address: www.lernerbooks.com

Library of Congress Cataloging-in-Publication Data

van Dyck, Sara.
   Bumblebees / by Sara van Dyck.
     p.   cm. — (Early bird nature books)
   Includes index.
   ISBN: 0–8225–2498–8 (lib. bdg. : alk. paper)
   1. Bumblebees—Juvenile literature. I. Title. II. Series.
QL568.A6V25 2005
595.79'9—dc22   2004019656

Manufactured in the United States of America
1 2 3 4 5 6 – JR – 10 09 08 07 06 05

Contents

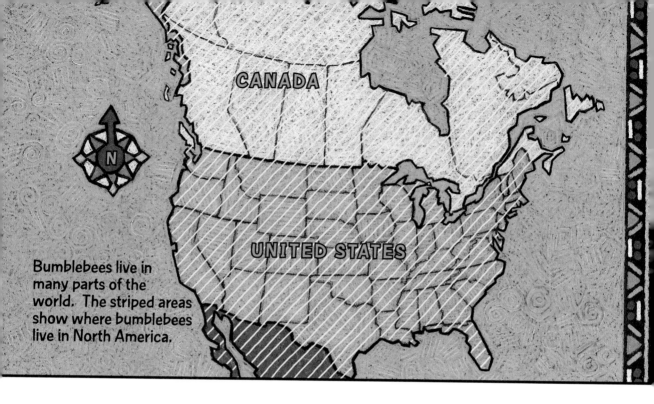

Bumblebees live in many parts of the world. The striped areas show where bumblebees live in North America.

CANADA

UNITED STATES

Be a Word Detective

Can you find these words as you read about the bumblebee's life? Be a detective and try to figure out what they mean. You can turn to the glossary on page 46 for help.

abdomen	honey stomach	pollen baskets
antennas	larvas	pollinated
colony	nectar	pupas
habitat	pollen	thorax

There is more than one way to form plurals of some words. The words antenna, larva, *and* pupa *have two possible plural endings—either with an e or an s. In this book, s is used when many* antennas, larvas, *and* pupas *are discussed.*

Chapter 1

The different parts of a bumblebee's body allow it to do many jobs. How many body parts do bumblebees have?

A Big, Buzzy Bee

Bumblebees are big, fuzzy insects. Like all insects, bumblebees have three main body parts. They have a head, a thorax, and an abodmen (AB-duh-muhn).

The head is at the front. The middle part is called the thorax. And the abdomen is at the back end of the bumblebee.

Two antennas (an-TEN-nuhs) grow out of a bumblebee's head. A bumblebee uses its antennas to smell things. It also has eyes on its head.

The three parts of a bumblebee's body can be seen in this photo.

Like other insects, bumblebees have six legs. Bumblebees also have two pairs of wings. Their front wings are bigger than their back wings. A bumblebee's legs and wings grow from its thorax.

In just one second, a bumblebee can beat its wings more than 100 times.

Shrews are one enemy of bumblebees. This shrew is trying to eat the bumblebee. But the bumblebee is stinging the shrew's nose.

A bumblebee's stinger is at the back of its abdomen. A bumblebee uses its stinger to fight off enemies.

A bumblebee's antennas send signals to its brain. The signals tell the bumblebee where a smell is coming from.

Some bumblebees can grow as big as 1 inch long. That is about the size of a jelly bean.

Bumblebees have thick yellow and black hair. The thick hair helps to keep them warm in cold weather.

But sometimes the weather gets too cold. When it's too cold, bumblebees can't fly. Then they shiver. When you get cold, your body shivers too. That makes your body warmer. A bumblebee makes its thorax shiver. Shivering warms up the bumblebee. Then it can fly.

A bumblebee uses its thorax to warm up. It also uses its thorax to cool off on hot days.

Chapter 2

Bumblebees live in many parts of the world. But they always live near flowers. Where do bumblebees live?

Bumblebees and Flowers

Bumblebees live in many different kinds of places. The kind of place where an animal lives is called its habitat (HAB-uh-tat). Bumblebees have lived in North America for millions of years.

Bumblebees live where flowers grow. Bumblebee food comes from flowers. Bumblebees land on flowers to look for food called nectar. Nectar is a sweet liquid that flowers make.

You can see through a bumblebee's wings.

This bumblebee uses its long tongue to get nectar from a flower.

A bumblebee's long, reddish tongue can reach deep into flowers to get the nectar. The end of a bumblebee's tongue is hairy. The hairs soak up the nectar. Then the nectar goes into the bumblebee's honey stomach. This is where a bumblebee stores nectar. The honey stomach is in the bumblebee's abdomen.

The bright yellow powder on this flower is pollen.

Bumblebees don't just look for nectar. They also take pollen from flowers. Pollen is a yellow or orange powder that flowers make. When a bumblebee lands on a flower, pollen sticks to the hairs on the bee's body.

The hairs on a bumblebee's leg work like tiny combs and brushes.

A bumblebee has tiny hairs on its legs. They are shaped like combs and brushes. The bumblebee uses the combs and brushes to gather a flower's pollen.

This bumblebee is gathering lots of pollen. The pollen is stored in the bee's pollen baskets.

Then the bumblebee stores the pollen in its pollen baskets. A bumblebee has one pollen basket on each back leg. When pollen baskets are full, they look like little golden bags.

Chapter 3

The hairs on this bumblebee are covered with pollen. What happens when a bumblebee carries pollen from one flower to another?

Special Bees for Special Jobs

Bumblebees move from flower to flower. Some of the flowers' pollen is left on the bumblebee's leg hairs. The pollen sticks to the next flower the bee visits. When this happens, the flower is pollinated.

18

Only pollinated flowers can make seeds. And seeds grow into new plants. Flowers need to get pollen from other flowers. Bumblebees bring this pollen to flowers.

These flowers need help from bumblebees.

Bumblebees can do special jobs that other bees can't do. For example, the red clover flower has its nectar hidden deep inside. Other kinds of bees can't get nectar from clover flowers. Their tongues are too short to reach the nectar.

This bee is a honeybee. Honeybees can't do some of the jobs that bumblebees can do.

There are about 50 species, or kinds, of bumblebees in North America. This bumblebee's scientific name is Bombus impatiens. *It is good at pollinating blueberry flowers.*

But a bumblebee's long tongue can easily reach inside clover flowers. So a bumblebee can get the nectar hidden deep inside a clover flower.

Blueberries grow from flowers on blueberry bushes.
Bumblebees pollinate these flowers.

Some plants, such as tomatoes, cranberries, and blueberries, do not make nectar. So many bees don't visit them. But these plants do make pollen. Bumblebees take pollen from their flowers.

Tomato flowers give pollen only when they are shaken. Bumblebees get the pollen by doing a little dance. This is called buzz pollination.

This is a tomato flower. Getting pollen from tomato flowers takes extra work.

*This bumblebee is about to buzz pollinate
a tomato flower.*

First, the bumblebee flies around a flower.
The bumblebee buzzes as it flies. Then it grabs
part of the flower. The bumblebee shakes its
body and the flower for a few seconds. When
the bumblebee does this, its buzzing sound
gets higher.

24

Shaking the tomato flower loosens the pollen. The bumblebee gathers the pollen. Then it flies to the next tomato flower. Each time the bumblebee lands, it carries pollen from one tomato flower to another. Many flowers get pollinated. Tomatoes will grow from these flowers.

Tomatoes grow from pollinated tomato flowers.

Chapter 4

*A group of
bumblebees lives
together in a nest.
What is the group of
bees called?*

Life in the Nest

Bumblebees are called social insects.
Social insects live and work in groups. A group
of bees is called a colony. Each colony has
three kinds of bees. It has a queen, some
males, and lots of workers.

Queens start colonies in the springtime. A queen starts her colony by herself. She often looks for a hole in the ground to begin her nest. Or she might use an old mouse nest.

This queen has picked a place for her nest.

This queen bumblebee is laying her eggs on a ball of pollen.

A queen bumblebee gets pollen and nectar from flowers. Then she goes back to the nest. She makes a ball out of pollen. She lays her eggs on the ball. She lays about 12 eggs.

The queen makes a honey pot near her eggs. She makes the pot out of wax from her body. Then she puts nectar in it. When the queen gets hungry, she eats nectar from the honey pot.

The queen doesn't have to leave the nest to get food. She eats from the honey pot.

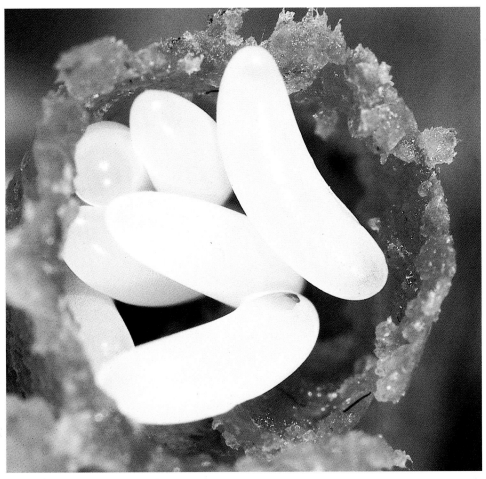

These are a bumblebee's eggs.

The queen covers her eggs with wax. Then she sits on the eggs to keep them warm. In four or five days, bumblebees hatch from the eggs. The babies are called larvas. The larvas feed on the pollen ball that the queen made.

The larvas grow for about a week. Then they change. The larvas become pupas. Each pupa covers itself with a cocoon. A cocoon is a silky case. The baby bee stays in its cocoon until it becomes an adult.

Bumblebee larvas look like fat, white worms.

These are bumblebee pupas.

About 10 days later, adult bees break out of their cocoons. The pupas have become worker bees.

The young worker bees fly from flower to flower, searching for pollen and nectar. They gather pollen and nectar. Then the worker bees bring the pollen and nectar back to the nest. The queen stays in the nest. She lays more eggs. She lays eggs all summer long.

An adult bumblebee is coming out of its cocoon.

Some workers stay in the nest with the queen. They help take care of the next set of eggs and larvas. Some workers build more pots to store nectar. But workers do not lay eggs. Soon the colony has all the workers it needs.

This worker bee is moving its wings like fans to cool the colony.

Some workers make pots to store nectar and pollen.

Late in the summer, young queens and males hatch. These queens and males do not do any work for the colony. Instead, they fly away together.

Each young queen eats a lot of nectar. She must fill up her honey stomach. The new queens need enough food for the winter. The young queens have eggs in their bodies. But they will not lay them until next spring. The young males die.

This young queen needs to store lots of nectar in her honey stomach.

Sometimes two queens fight each other.

When fall comes, the old queen and the workers die. The young queens find a place to stay during the cold weather. They stay there all winter in a kind of sleep. When spring comes, the bumblebee queens wake up. They find places for nests. They lay eggs. And they start new colonies.

Chapter 5

These tomatoes are growing in a greenhouse. Why do people grow plants in greenhouses?

Bumblebees and People

 Bumblebees help people to grow tomatoes in greenhouses. Greenhouses are heated buildings. They have a glass roof and sides. Plants can grow in greenhouses when it is too cold to grow outside.

People used to use machines to pollinate tomatoes in greenhouses. Then people learned that bumblebees do a fine job of pollinating indoor plants. Many people use bumblebees to do this job.

Some people build nests for bumblebee colonies.

Some people plant flowers to attract bumblebees to their yards.

Farmers from Europe went to New Zealand a long time ago. They planted red clover for their cows and sheep to eat. But the clover they planted did not make seeds. When the plants died, no new plants would grow. The cows and sheep would run out of food.

Then the farmers learned that New Zealand did not have any bumblebees. The farmers brought bumblebees from Europe. The bumblebees pollinated the clover. Pollination helped new clover plants to grow.

Clover flowers need to be pollinated by bumblebees.
Then new clover plants can grow.

This farmer is spraying a field to kill pests.
But sprays can kill bumblebees.

Farmers and gardeners need bumblebees.
But sometimes these people hurt the bees.
People don't mean to harm bumblebees. But
a farmer might destroy a colony while digging
up a field for planting. Sometimes people use
sprays on their plants to kill weeds and harmful
insects. The sprays often kill bumblebees too.

Two bumblebees drink from a honey pot.

People are often afraid that bumblebees will sting them. But bumblebees usually do not sting unless people or animals bother them. Bumblebees are really people's helpers.

On Sharing a Book

As you know, adults greatly influence a child's attitude toward reading. When a child sees you read, or when you share a book with a child, you're sending a message that reading is important. Show the child that reading a book together is important to you. Find a comfortable, quiet place. Turn off the television and limit other distractions, such as telephone calls.

Be prepared to start slowly. Take turns reading parts of this book. Stop and talk about what you're reading. Talk about the photographs. You may find that much of the shared time is spent discussing just a few pages. This discussion time is valuable for both of you, so don't move through the book too quickly. If the child begins to lose interest, stop reading. Continue sharing the book at another time. When you do pick up the book again, be sure to revisit the parts you have already read. Most importantly, enjoy the book!

Be a Vocabulary Detective

You will find a word list on page 5. Words selected for this list are important to the understanding of the topic of this book. Encourage the child to be a word detective and search for the words as you read the book together. Talk about what the words mean and how they are used in the sentence. Do any of these words have more than one meaning? You will find these words defined in a glossary on page 46.

What about Questions?

Use questions to make sure the child understands the information in this book. Here are some suggestions:

> What did this paragraph tell us? What does this picture show? What do you think we'll learn about next? Where do bumblebees live? Could a bumblebee live in your backyard? Why/Why not? How is your body different from a bumblebee's body? Where do bumblebees find their food? Why are bumblebees called social insects? How many stages does a bumblebee go through to become an adult? What is your favorite part of this book? Why?

If the child has questions, don't hesitate to respond with questions of your own, such as What do *you* think? Why? What is it that you don't know? If the child can't remember certain facts, turn to the index.

Introducing the Index

The index is an important learning tool. It helps readers get information quickly without searching throughout the whole book. Turn to the index on page 47. Choose an entry, such as *tongue*, and ask the child to use the index to find out how a bumblebee uses its tongue to get food. Repeat this exercise with as many entries as you like. Ask the child to point out the differences between an index and a glossary. (The index helps readers find information quickly, while the glossary tells readers what words mean.)

Where in the World?

Many plants and animals found in the Early Bird Nature Books series live in parts of the world other than the United States. Encourage the child to find the places mentioned in this book on a world map or globe. Take time to talk about climate, terrain, and how you might live in such places.

All the World in Metric!

Although our monetary system is in metric units (based on multiples of 10), the United States is one of the few countries in the world that does not use the metric system of measurement. Here are some conversion activities you and the child can do using a calculator:

WHEN YOU KNOW:	MULTIPLY BY:	TO FIND:
miles	1.609	kilometers
feet	0.3048	meters
inches	2.54	centimeters
gallons	3.785	liters
tons	0.907	metric tons
pounds	0.454	kilograms

Activities

Make up a story about a bumblebee. Be sure to include information from this book. Draw or paint pictures to illustrate your story.

Go into your yard or visit a park where flowers grow. Find the pollen in three different kinds of flowers. Is the pollen always the same color?

Act out being a bumblebee. Where do you live? How do you get food? If you were a queen bumblebee, what would your special job be? Draw a picture of your colony.

Glossary

abdomen (AB-duh-muhn): the back part of a bumblebee's body

antennas (an-TEN-nuhs): the feelers on a bumblebee's head

colony: a group of bumblebees that live together

habitat (HAB-uh-tat): an area where a kind of animal can live and grow

honey stomach: the part of a bumblebee's body that stores nectar from flowers

larvas: bumblebees in their second stage of growth

nectar: the sweet liquid that flowers make

pollen: the yellow or orange powder that flowers use to make seeds

pollen baskets: parts of a bumblebee's back legs that the bee uses to carry pollen

pollinated: pollen from one flower moved to another flower so the second flower can make seeds

pupas: bumblebees in their third stage of growth

thorax: the middle part of a bumblebee's body

Index

Pages listed in **bold** type refer to photographs.

About the Author

Sara van Dyck, who has a bachelor's degree in science and a master's degree in education, taught for fifteen years. Her lifelong fascination with nature and the environment is reflected in her book, *Insect Wars,* and in her magazine articles for adults and children. She has spoken many times at schools and libraries about the importance of insects to the environment. She lives in Santa Monica, California, with her husband.